The **Prophet** *and the* **Plates**

The **Prophet** *and the* **Plates**

Oliver Cowdery

on the Events of the Restoration

TEMPLE HILL

The picture on the cover was discovered by Patrick A. Bishop in the Library of Congress Archives in Washington, D.C. For more information, see "An Original Daguerreotype of Oliver Cowdery Identified," *BYU Studies,* vol. 45, no. 2, 2006, 100–111.

The views expressed in this book are the responsibility of the author and do not necessarily represent the position of The Editorium. The reader alone is responsible for the use of any ideas or information provided by this book.

ISBN 1-60096-540-7

Published by Temple Hill Books, an imprint of The Editorium

Temple Hill Books™, the Temple Hill Books logo, and The Editorium™ are trademarks of The Editorium, LLC

The Editorium, LLC
West Valley City, UT 84128-3917
templehillbooks.com
templehill@editorium.com

Contents

Publisher's Preface

The Prophet and the Plates is a collection of letters from Oliver Cowdery to W. W. Phelps for publication in the Latter-day Saint newspaper *The Messenger and Advocate.* They include Oliver's recollections of events related to the restoration of the gospel and the translation of the Book of Mormon, and they constitute the earliest printed account of the birth of Mormonism.

The October 1834 issue of *The Messenger and Advocate* announced that the paper would publish "a full history" of the Church in installments (see the introduction to this volume), noting, "Our brother J. SMITH jr. has offered to assist us." Eventually eight letters were published.

In letter 1, Oliver describes meeting Joseph Smith in April 1829, when he began serving as the Prophet's scribe for the translation of the Book of Mormon. During the translation, they prayed to know concerning the authority to baptize, leading to the appearance of an angel who conferred upon them the priesthood of Aaron. (*Messenger and Advocate* 1, no. 1 [October 1834]: 13–16.)

Letter 2 explains the universal apostasy and the rejection of prophets because of their imperfections. (*Messenger and Advocate* 1, no. 2 [November 1834]: 27–32.)

A letter from Joseph Smith gives the circumstances of his early life and explains the "vices and follies" of his youth. (*Messenger and Advocate* 1, no. 3 [December 1834]: 41.)

Letter 3 describes the religious "excitement" that existed during Joseph's youth and his uncertainty over which church to join. (*Messenger and Advocate* 1, no. 3 [December 1834]: 41–43.)

Letter 4 recounts the visit of the Angel Moroni, who told Joseph that his sins were forgiven and that the Lord had a marvelous work to perform through him. (*Messenger and Advocate* 1, no. 5 [February 1835]: 77–80.)

Letter 5 includes Oliver's arguments for the necessity of the Restoration and the Gathering. (*Messenger and Advocate* 1, no. 5 [February 1835]: 77–80.)

Letter 6 explains the Restoration's fulfillment of Old Testament prophecies. (*Messenger and Advocate* 1, no. 7 [April 1835]: 108–12.)

Letter 7 describes Joseph's temptation to obtain the plates for monetary gain and the appearance and significance of the Hill Cumorah. (*Messenger and Advocate* 1, no. 10 [July 1835]: 155–59.)

Letter 8 describes the burial of the Nephite artifacts, Joseph's acquisition of the gold plates, and a defense of the Prophet's character. (*Messenger and Advocate* 2, no. 1 [October 1835]: 195–202.)

As needed, punctuation and spelling have been modernized for easier reading.

Introduction

The following communication was designed to have been published in the last No. of the [*Millennial*] *Star,* but owing to a press of other matter it was laid over for this No. of the *Messenger and Advocate.* Since it was written, upon further reflection, we have thought that a full history of the rise of the church of the Latter Day Saints, and the most interesting parts of its progress to the present time, would be worthy the perusal of the saints. If circumstances admit, an article on this subject will appear in each subsequent No. of the *Messenger and Advocate,* until the time when the church was driven from Jackson Co. Mo. by a lawless banditti; and such other remarks as may be thought appropriate and interesting.

That our narrative may be correct, and particularly the introduction, it is proper to inform our patrons that our brother J. SMITH jr. has offered to assist us. Indeed, there are many items connected with the fore part of this subject that render his labor indispensable. With his labor and with authentic documents now in our possession,[1] we hope to render this a pleasing and agreeable narrative, well worth the examination and perusal of the saints. To do justice to this subject will require time and space: we therefore ask

---

1. Probably including Joseph Smith's 1832 history.

the forbearance of our readers, assuring them that it shall be founded upon facts.

Letter 1

Norton, Medina co. Ohio, Sabbath evening, September 7, 1834.

DEAR BROTHER, Before leaving home, I promised, if I tarried long, to write; and while a few moments are now allowed me for reflection, aside from the cares and common conversation of my friends in this place, I have thought that were I to communicate them to you, might, perhaps, if they should not prove especially beneficial to yourself, by confirming you in the faith of the gospel, at least be interesting, since it has pleased our heavenly Father to call us both to rejoice in the same hope of eternal life. And by giving them publicity, some thousands who have embraced the same covenant, may learn something more particular upon the rise of this church, in this last time. And while the gray evening is fast changing into a settled darkness, my heart responds with the happy millions who are in the presence of the Lamb, and are past the power of temptation, in rendering thanks, though feebly, to the same Parent.

Another day has passed, into that, to us, boundless ocean, ETERNITY! where nearly six thousand years have gone before; and what flits across the mind like an electric shock is that it will never return! Whether it has been well improved or not; whether the principles emanating from HIM who "hallowed" it have been observed; or whether, like the common mass of time, it has been heedlessly spent, is not for me to say. One thing I can say: It can never be recalled! It has rolled in to assist in filling up the grand space decreed in the mind of its Author, till nature shall have ceased her work, and time its accustomed revolutions—when its Lord shall have completed the gathering of his elect, and with them enjoy that Sabbath which shall never end!

On Friday, the 5th, in company with our brother JOSEPH SMITH jr., I left Kirtland for this place (New Portage) to attend the conference previously appointed. To be permitted, once more, to travel with this brother occasions reflections of no ordinary kind. Many have been the fatigues and privations which have fallen to my lot to endure, for the gospel's sake, since 1828, with this brother. Our road has frequently been spread with the "fowler's snare," and our persons sought with the eagerness of the Savage's ferocity for innocent blood, by men either heated to desperation by the insinuations of those who professed to be "guides and way-marks" to the kingdom of glory, or the individuals themselves! This, I confess, is a dark picture to spread before our patrons, but they will pardon my plainness when I assure them of the truth. In fact, God has so ordered that the reflections which I am permitted to cast upon my past life, relative to a knowledge of the way of salvation, are rendered "doubly endearing." Not only have I been graciously preserved from wicked and unreasonable men with this our brother, but I have seen the fruit of perseverance in proclaiming the everlasting gospel, immediately after it was declared to the world in these last days, in a manner not to be forgotten while heaven gives my common intellect. And what serves to render the reflection past expression on this point is that from his hand I received baptism, by the direction of the angel of God—the first received into this church, in this day.

Near the time of the setting of the Sun, Sabbath evening, April 5th, 1829, my natural eyes for the first time beheld this brother. He then resided in Harmony, Susquehanna County, Penn. On Monday the 6th, I assisted him in arranging some business of a temporal nature, and on Tuesday the 7th, commenced to write the Book of Mormon. These were days never to be forgotten—to sit under the sound of a voice dictated by the inspiration of heaven awakened the utmost gratitude of this bosom! Day after day I continued, uninterrupted, to write from his mouth, as he translated, with the Urim and Thummim—or, as the Nephites would have said, "Interpreters"—the history, or record, called "The book of Mormon."

To notice, in even few words, the interesting account given by Mormon, and his faithful son Moroni, of a people once beloved and favored of heaven, would supersede my present design: I shall therefore defer this to a future period, and as I said in the introduction, pass more directly to some few incidents immediately connected with the rise of this church, which may be entertaining to some thousands who have stepped forward, amid the frowns of bigots and the calumny of hypocrites, and embraced the gospel of Christ.

No men in their sober senses could translate and write the directions given to the Nephites, from the mouth of the Savior, of the precise manner in which men should build up his church, and especially, when corruption had spread an uncertainty over all forms and systems practiced among men, without desiring a privilege of showing the willingness of the heart by being buried in the liquid grave, to answer a "good conscience by the resurrection of Jesus Christ."

After writing the account given of the Savior's ministry to the remnant of the seed of Jacob upon this continent, it was easily to be seen, as the prophet said would be, that darkness covered the earth and gross darkness the minds of the people. On reflecting further, it was as easily to be seen, that amid the great strife and noise concerning religion, none had authority from God to administer the ordinances of the gospel. For, the question might be asked, have men authority to administer in the name of Christ, who deny revelations? when his testimony is no less than the spirit of prophecy? and his religion based, built, and sustained by immediate revelations in all ages of the world, when he has had a people on earth? If these facts were buried, and carefully concealed by men whose craft would have been in danger, if once permitted to shine in the faces of men, they were no longer to us; and we only waited for the commandment to be given, "Arise and be baptized."

This was not long desired before it was realized. The Lord, who is rich in mercy, and ever willing to answer the consistent prayer of the humble, after we had called upon him in a fervent manner, aside from the abodes of men, condescended to manifest to us his will. On a sudden, as from the midst of eternity, the voice of the Redeemer spake peace to us, while the veil was parted and the angel of God came down clothed with glory, and delivered the anxiously looked for message, and the keys of the gospel of repentance! What joy! what wonder! what amazement! While the world were racked and distracted— while millions were groping as the blind for the wall, and while all men were resting upon uncertainty, as a general mass, our eyes beheld—our ears heard. As in the "blaze of day"; yes, more—above the glitter of the May sunbeam, which then shed its brilliancy over the face of nature! Then his voice, though mild, pierced to the center, and his words,

"I am thy fellow servant," dispelled every fear. We listened—we gazed—we admired! 'Twas the voice of the angel from glory—'twas a message from the Most High! and as we heard we rejoiced, while his love enkindled upon our souls, and we were rapt in the vision of the Almighty! Where was room for doubt? Nowhere: uncertainty had fled, doubt had sunk, no more to rise, while fiction and deception had fled forever!

But, dear brother think, further think for a moment, what joy filled our hearts and with what surprise we must have bowed (for who would not have bowed the knee for such a blessing?) when we received under his hand the holy priesthood, as he said, "Upon you my fellow servants, in the name of Messiah I confer this priesthood and this authority, which shall remain upon earth, that the sons of Levi may yet offer an offering unto the Lord in righteousness!"[1]

---

1. Oliver later wrote on October 21, 1848, "The priesthood is here. I was present with Joseph when an holy angel from God came down from heaven and conferred or restored the Aaronic priesthood. And said at the same time that it should remain upon the earth while the earth stands. I was also present with Joseph when the Melchizedek priesthood was conferred by the holy angels of God—this was the more necessary in order that which we then confirmed on each other by the will and commandment of God. This priesthood is also to remain upon the earth until the last remnant of time." (In Joseph Smith, *History of The Church of Jesus Christ of Latter-day Saints*, 7 vols. 2d ed. rev., edited by B. H. Roberts [Salt Lake City: The Church of Jesus Christ of Latter-day Saints, 1932–51], 1: 40.)

On March 23, 1846, he wrote to Phineas H. Young, "I have cherished a hope, and that one of my fondest, that I might leave such a character as those who might believe in my testimony, after I shall be called hence, might do so, not only for the sake of the truth, but might not blush for the private character of the man who bore that testimony. I have been sensitive on this subject, I admit; but I ought to be so—you would be, under the circumstances, had you stood in the presence of John, with our departed brother Joseph, to receive the Lesser Priesthood—and in the presence of Peter, to receive the Greater, and look down through time, and

I shall not attempt to paint to you the feelings of this heart, nor the majestic beauty and glory which surrounded us on this occasion; but you will believe me when I say that earth, nor men, with the eloquence of time, cannot begin to clothe language in as interesting and sublime a manner as this holy personage. No; nor has this earth power to give the joy, to bestow the peace, or comprehend the wisdom which was contained in each sentence as they were delivered by the power of the Holy Spirit! Man may deceive his fellow man; deception may follow deception, and the children of the wicked one may have power to seduce the foolish and untaught, till naught but fiction feeds the many, and the fruit of falsehood carries in its current the giddy to the grave; but one touch with the finger of his love, yes, one ray of glory from the upper world, or one word from the mouth of the Savior, from the bosom of eternity, strikes it all into insignificance, and blots it forever from the mind! The assurance that we were in the presence of an angel; the certainty that we heard the voice of Jesus, and the truth unsullied as it flowed from a pure personage, dictated by the will of God, is to me, past description, and I shall ever look upon this expression of the Savior's goodness with wonder and thanksgiving while I am permitted to tarry, and in those mansions where perfection dwells and sin never comes, I hope to adore in that DAY which shall never cease! (I will hereafter give you a full history of the rise of this church, up to the time stated in my introduction; which will necessarily embrace the life and character of this brother. I shall therefore leave the history of baptism, etc., till its proper place.) . . .

---

witness the effects these two must produce." (Letter of Oliver Cowdery to Phineas H. Young, March 23, 1846, Tiffin, Ohio, Oliver Cowdery Papers, 1835–1849, LDS Church Archives.)

I must close for the present: my candle is quite extinguished, and all nature seems locked in silence, shrouded in darkness, and enjoying that repose so necessary to this life. But the period is rolling on when night will close, and those who are found worthy will inherit that city where neither the light of the sun nor moon will be necessary! "for the glory of God will lighten it, and the Lamb will be the light thereof."

O. Cowdery.

To W. W. PHELPS, Esq.

. . .

Letter 2

To W. W. Phelps, Esq.

DEAR BROTHER: In the last *Messenger and Advocate* I promised to commence a more particular or minute history of the rise and progress of the church of the Latter Day Saints; and publish, for the benefit of inquirers, and all who are disposed to learn. There are certain facts relative to the works of God worthy the consideration and observance of every individual, and every society: They are that he never works in the dark—his works are always performed in a clear, intelligible manner: and another point is that he never works in vain. This is not the case with men; but might it not be? When the Lord works, he accomplishes his purposes, and the effects of his power are to be seen afterward. In view of this, suffer me to make a few remarks by way of introduction. The works of man may shine for a season with a degree of brilliancy, but time changes their complexion; and whether it did or not, all would be the same in a little space, as nothing except that which was erected by a hand which never grows weak can remain when corruption is consumed.

I shall not be required to adorn and beautify my narrative with a relation of the faith of ENOCH, and those who assisted him to build up Zion, which fled to God—on the mountains of which was commanded the blessing, life forever more—to be held in reserve to add another ray of glory to the grand retinue, when worlds shall rock from their base to their center; the nations of the righteous rise from the dust, and the blessed millions of the church of the first born shout his triumphant coming, to receive his kingdom, over which he is to reign till all enemies are subdued.

Nor shall I write the history of the Lord's church, raised up according to his own instruction to Moses and Aaron; of the perplexities and discouragements which came upon Israel for their transgressions; their organization upon the land of Canaan, and their overthrow and dispersion among all nations, to reap the reward of their iniquities, to the appearing of the Great Shepherd in the flesh.

But there is, of necessity, a uniformity so exact, a manner so precise, and ordinances so minute, in all ages and generations whenever God has established his church among men, that should I have occasion to recur to either age, and particularly to that characterized by the advent of the Messiah, and the ministry of the apostles of that church; with a cursory view of the same till it lost its visibility on earth; was driven into darkness, or till God took the holy priesthood unto himself, where it has been held in reserve to the present century, as a matter of right, in this free country, I may take the privilege. This may be doubted by some—indeed by many—as an admission of this point would overthrow the popular systems of the day. I cannot reasonably expect, then, that the large majority of professors will be willing to listen to my argument for a moment, as a careful, impartial, and faithful investigation of the doctrines which I believe to be correct, and the principles cherished in my bosom—and believed by this church—by every honest man must be admitted as truth. Of this I may say as Tertullian said to the Emperor when writing in defense of the saints in his day: "Whoever looked well into our religion that did not embrace it?"

Common undertakings and plans of men may be overthrown or destroyed by opposition. The systems of this world may be exploded or annihilated by oppression or falsehood; but it is the reverse with pure religion. There is a power attendant on truth that all the arts and designs of men cannot fathom; there is an increasing influence which rises up in one place the moment it is covered in another, and the more it is traduced, and the harsher the means employed to effect its extinction, the more numerous are its votaries. It is not the vain cry of "delusion" from the giddy multitude; it is not the sneers of bigots; it is not the frowns of zealots, neither the rage of princes, kings, nor emperors, that can prevent its influence. The fact is, as Tertullian said, no man ever looked carefully into its consistency and propriety without embracing it. It is impossible: That light which enlightens man, is at once enraptured; that intelligence which existed before the world was, will unite, and that wisdom in the Divine economy will be so conspicuous, that it will be embraced, it will be observed, and it must be obeyed!

Look at pure religion whenever it has had a place on earth, and you will always mark the same characteristics in all its features. Look at truth (without which the former could not exist), and the same peculiarities are apparent. Those who have been guided by them have always shown the same principles; and those who were not, have as uniformly sought to destroy their influence. Religion has had its friends and its enemies; its advocates and its opponents. But the thousands of years which have come and gone, have left it unaltered; the millions who have embraced it, and are now enjoying that bliss held forth in its promises, have left its principles unchanged, and its influence upon the honest heart, unweakened. The many oppositions which have encountered it; the millions of calumnies, the numberless reproaches, and the myriads of falsehoods, have left its fair form unimpaired, its beauty untarnished, and its excellence as excellent; while its certainty is the same, and its foundation upheld by the hand of God!

One peculiarity of men I wish to notice in the early part of my narrative. So far as my acquaintance and knowledge of men and their history extends, it has been the custom of every generation, to boast of, or extol the acts of the former. In this respect I wish it to be distinctly understood, that I mean the righteous—those to whom God communicated his will. There has ever been an apparent blindness common to men, which has hindered their discovering the real worth and excellence of individuals while residing with them; but when once deprived of their society, worth, and counsel, they were ready to exclaim, "how great and inestimable were their qualities, and how precious is their memory."

The vilest and most corrupt are not exempted from this charge: even the Jews, whose former principles had become degenerated, and whose religion was a mere show, were found among that class who were ready to build and garnish the sepulchers of the prophets, and condemn their fathers for putting them to death; making important boasts of their own righteousness, and of their assurance of salvation, in the midst of which they rose up with one consent, and treacherously and shamefully betrayed, and crucified the Savior of the world! No wonder that the inquirer has turned aside with disgust, nor marvel that God has appointed a day when he will call the nations before him, and reward every man according to his works!

Enoch walked with God, and was taken home without tasting death. Why were not all converted in his day and taken with him to glory? Noah, it is said, was perfect in his generation; and it is plain that he had communion with his Maker, and by HIS direction accomplished a work the parallel of which is not to be found in the annals of the world! Why were not the world converted, that the flood might have been stayed? Men, from the days of our father Abraham, have talked, boasted, and extolled his faith: and he is even represented in the scriptures "The father of the faithful." Moses talked with the Lord face to face; received the great moral law, upon the basis of which those of all civilized governments are founded; led Israel forty years, and was taken home to receive the reward of his toils—then Jacob could realize his worth. Well was the question asked by our Lord, "How can the children of the bridechamber mourn while the bridegroom is with them?" It is said, that he traveled and taught the righteous principles of his kingdom, three years, during which he chose twelve men, and ordained them apostles, etc. The people saw and heard—they were particularly benefited, many of them, by being healed of infirmities, and diseases; of plagues, and devils: they saw him walk upon the water; they saw the winds and waves calmed at his command; they saw thousands fed to the full with a pittance, and the very powers of darkness tremble in his presence—and like others before them, considered it as a dream, or a common occurrence, till the time was fulfilled, and he was offered up. Yet while he was with them he said, you shall desire to see one of the days of the Son of Man, and shall not see it. He knew that calamity would fall upon that people, and the wrath of heaven overtake them to their overthrow; and when that devoted city was surrounded with armies, well may we conclude that they desired a protector possessing sufficient power to lead them to some safe place aside from the tumult of a siege.

Since the apostles fell asleep all men who profess a belief in the truth of their mission, extol their virtues and celebrate their fame. It seems to have been forgotten that they were men of infirmities and subject to all the feelings, passions, and imperfections common to other men. But it appears, that they, as others were before them, are looked upon as men of perfection, holiness, purity, and goodness, far in advance of any since. So were the characters of the prophets held in the days of these apostles. What can be the difference in the reward, whether a man died for righteousness' sake in the days of Abel, Zacharias, John, the twelve apostles chosen at Jerusalem, or since? Is not the life of one equally as precious as the other? and is not the truth, just as true?

But in reviewing the lives and acts of men in past generations, whenever we find a righteous man among them, there always were excuses for not giving heed or credence to his testimony. The people could see his imperfections; or, if no imperfections, supposed ones, and were always ready to frame an excuse upon that for not believing. No matter how pure the principles, nor how precious the teachings—an excuse was wanted—and an excuse was had.

The next generation, perhaps, was favored with equally as righteous men, who were condemned upon the same principles of the former, while the acts and precepts of the former were the boasts of the multitude; when, in reality, their doctrines were no more pure, their exertions to turn men to righteousness no greater, neither their walk any more circumspect—the grave of the former is considered to be holy, and his sepulcher is garnished while the latter is deprived a dwelling among men, or even an existence upon earth! Such is a specimen of the depravity and inconsistency of men, and such has been their conduct toward the righteous in centuries past.

When John the son of Zacharias came among the Jews, it is said that he came neither eating bread nor drinking wine. In another place it is said that his meat was locusts and wild honey. The Jews saw him, heard him preach, and were witnesses of the purity of the doctrines advocated—they wanted an excuse, and they soon found one—"He hath a devil!"—And who, among all generations, that valued his salvation, would be taught by, or follow one possessed of a devil?

The Savior came in form and fashion of a man; he ate, drank, and walked about as a man, and they said, "Behold, a man gluttonous, and a winebibber, a friend of publicans and sinners!" You see an excuse was wanting, but not long wanting till it was found—Who would follow a dissipated leader? or who, among the righteous Pharisees would acknowledge a man who would condescend to eat with publicans and sinners? This was too much—they could not endure it. An individual teaching the doctrines of the kingdom of heaven, and declaring that that kingdom was nigh, or that it had already come, must appear different from others, or he could not be received. If he were athirst he must not drink, if faint he must not eat, and if weary he must not rest, because he had assumed the authority to teach the world righteousness, and he must be different in manners, and in constitution, if not in form, that all might be attracted by his singular appearance: that his singular demeanor might gain the reverence of the people, or he was an impostor—a false teacher—a wicked man—a sinner—and an accomplice of Beelzebub, the prince of devils!

If singularity of appearance, or difference of manners would command respect, certainly John would have been reverenced, and heard. To see one coming from the wilderness, clad with camels' hair, drinking neither wine nor strong drink, nor yet eating common food, must have awakened the curiosity of the curious, to the fullest extent. But there was one peculiarity in this man common to every righteous man before him, for which the people hated him, and for which he lost his life—he taught holiness, proclaimed repentance and baptism for the remission of sins, warned the people of the consequences of iniquity, and declared that the kingdom of heaven was at hand. All this was too much! To see one dressed so ridiculously, eating no common food, neither drinking wine like other men; stepping in advance of the learned and reverend Pharisees, wise doctors, and righteous scribes, and declaring, at the same time, that the Lord's kingdom would soon appear, could not be borne—he must not teach—he must not assume—he must not attempt to lead the people after him—"He hath a devil!"

The Jews were willing (professedly so) to believe the ancient prophets, and follow the directions of heaven as delivered to the world by them; but when one came teaching the same doctrine, and proclaiming the same things, only that they were nearer, they would not hear. Men say if they could see they would believe; but I have thought the reverse, in this respect—If they cannot see they will believe.

One of two reasons may be assigned as the cause why the messengers of truth have been rejected—perhaps both. The multitude saw their imperfections, or supposed ones, and from that framed an excuse for rejecting them; or else in consequence of the corruption of their own hearts, when reproved, were not willing to repent; but sought to make a man an offender for a word: or for wearing camels' hair, eating locusts, drinking wine, or showing friendship to publicans and sinners!

When looking over the sacred scriptures, we seem to forget that they were given through men of imperfections, and subject to passions. It is a general belief that the ancient prophets were perfect—that no stain, or blemish ever appeared upon their characters while on earth, to be brought forward by the opposer as an excuse for not believing. The same is said of the apostles; but James said that Elias [Elijah] was a man subject to like passions as themselves, and yet he had that power with God that in answer to his prayer it rained not on the earth by the space of three years and a half.

There can be no doubt but those to whom he wrote looked upon the ancient prophets as a race of beings superior to any in those days; and in order to be constituted a prophet of God, a man must be perfect in every respect. The idea is, that he must be perfect according to their signification of the word. If a people were blessed with prophets, they must be the individuals who were to prescribe the laws by which they must be governed, even in their private walks. The generation following were ready to suppose, that those men who believed the word of God were as perfect as those to whom it was delivered supposed they must be, and were as forward to prescribe the rules by which they were governed, or rehearse laws and declare them to be the governing principles of the prophets, as though they themselves held the keys of the mysteries of heaven, and had searched the archives of the generations of the world.

You will see that I have made mention of the Messiah, of his mission into the world, and of his walk and outward appearance; but do not understand me as attempting to place him on a level with men, or his mission on a parallel with those of the prophets and apostles—far from this. I view his mission such as none other could fill; that he was offered without spot to God a propitiation for our sins; that he rose triumphant, and victorious over the grave and him that has the power of death. This, man could not do—It required a perfect sacrifice—man is imperfect—It required a spotless offering—man is not spotless—It required an infinite atonement—man is mortal!

I have, then, as you will see, made mention of our Lord, to show that individuals teaching truth, whether perfect or imperfect, have been looked upon as the worst of men. And that even our Savior, the great Shepherd of Israel, was mocked and derided, and placed on a parallel with the prince of devils; and the prophets and apostles, though at this day, looked upon as perfect as perfection, were considered the basest of the human family by those among whom they lived. It is not rumor, though it is wafted by every gale, and reiterated by every zephyr, upon which we are to found our judgments of one's merits or demerits: If it is, we erect an altar upon which we sacrifice the most perfect of men, and establish a criterion by which the "vilest of the vile" may escape censure.

But lest I weary you with too many remarks upon the history of the past, after a few upon the propriety of a narrative of the description I have proposed, I shall proceed.—Editor.

Letter from Joseph Smith

BROTHER O. COWDERY:

Having learned from the first No. of the *Messenger and Advocate,* that you were not only about to "give a history of the rise and progress of the church of the Latter Day Saints," but that said "history would necessarily embrace my life and character," I have been induced to give you the time and place of my birth; as I have learned that many of the opposers of those principles which I have held forth to the world profess a personal acquaintance with me, though when in my presence, represent me to be another person in age, education, and stature from what I am.

I was born (according to the record of the same, kept by my parents) in the town of Sharon, Windsor Co., Vt. on the 23rd of December, 1805.

At the age of ten my father's family removed to Palmyra, N.Y., where, and in the vicinity of which I lived, or made it my place of residence, until I was twenty-one, the latter part in the town of Manchester.

During this time, as is common to most, or all youths, I fell into many vices and follies; but as my accusers are, and have been forward to accuse me of being guilty of gross and outrageous violations of the peace and good order of the community, I take the occasion to remark that though, as I

19

have said above, "as is common to most, or all youths, I fell into many vices and follies," I have not, neither can it be sustained, in truth, been guilty of wronging or injuring any man or society of men; and those imperfections to which I allude, and for which I have often had occasion to lament, were a light and too often vain mind, exhibiting a foolish and trifling conversation.

This being all, and the worst, that my accusers can substantiate against my moral character, I wish to add that it is not without a deep feeling of regret that I am thus called upon in answer to my own conscience, to fulfill a duty I owe to myself, as well as to the cause of truth, in making this public confession of my former uncircumspect walk and unchaste conversation: and more particularly, as I often acted in violation of those holy precepts which I knew came from God. But as the "Articles and Covenants" of this church are plain upon this particular point, I do not deem it important to proceed further. I only add that I do not, nor never have, pretended to be any other than a man "subject to passion," and liable, without the assisting grace of the Savior, to deviate from that perfect path in which all men are commanded to walk!

By giving the above a place in your valuable paper, you will confer a lasting favor upon myself, as an individual, and, as I humbly hope, subserve the cause of righteousness.

I am, with feelings of esteem, your fellow laborer in the gospel of our Lord.

JOSEPH SMITH jr.

Letter 3

TO W. W. Phelps, Esq.

DEAR BROTHER:

After a silence of another month, agreeably to my promise, I proceed upon the subject I proposed in the first No. of the *Advocate*. Perhaps an apology for brevity may not be improper here, as many important incidents consequently transpiring in the organization and establishing of a society like the one whose history I am about to give to the world are overlooked or lost, and soon buried with those who were the actors, will prevent my giving those minute and particular reflections which I have so often wished might have characterized the "Acts of the apostles" and the ancient saints. But such facts as are within my knowledge will be given without any reference to inconsistencies in the minds of others, or impossibilities in the feelings of such as do not give credence to the system of salvation and redemption so clearly set forth and so plainly written over the face of the sacred scriptures.

Upon the propriety, then, of a narrative of this kind, I have briefly to remark: It is known to you that this church has suffered reproach and persecution from a majority of mankind, who have heard but a rumor since its first organization. And further, you are also conversant with the fact that no sooner had the messengers of the fullness of the gospel begun to proclaim its heavenly precepts, and call upon men to embrace the same, than they were vilified and slandered by thousands who never saw their faces, and much less knew aught derogatory of their characters, moral or religious. Upon this unfair and unsaintlike manner of procedure they have been giving in large sheets their own opinions of the incorrectness of our system, and attested volumes of our lives and characters.

Since, then, our opposers have been thus kind to introduce our cause before the public, it is no more than just that a correct account should be given; and since they have invariably sought to cast a shade over the truth, and hinder its influence from gaining ascendancy, it is also proper that it should be vindicated, by laying before the world a correct statement of events as they have transpired from time to time.

Whether I shall succeed so far in my purpose as to convince the public of the incorrectness of those scurrilous reports which have inundated our land, or even but a small portion of them, will be better ascertained when I close than when I commence; and I am content to submit it before the candid for perusal, and before the Judge of all for inspection, as I most assuredly believe that before HIM I must stand and answer for the deeds transacted in this life.

Should I, however, be instrumental in causing a few to hear before they judge, and understand both sides of this matter before they condemn, I shall have the satisfaction of seeing them embrace it, as I am certain that one is the inevitable fruit of the other. But to proceed:

You will recollect that I informed you, in my letter published in the first No. of the *Messenger and Advocate,* that this history would necessarily embrace the life and character of our esteemed friend and brother, J. Smith Jr. one of the presidents of this church, and for information on that part of the subject, I refer you to his communication of the same published in this paper. I shall, therefore, pass over that, till I come to the 15th year of his life.

It is necessary to premise this account by relating the situation of the public mind relative to religion at this time: One Mr. Lane, a presiding Elder of the Methodist church, visited Palmyra and vicinity. Elder Lane was a talented man possessing a good share of literary endowments, and apparent humility. There was a great awakening, or excitement, raised on the subject of religion, and much inquiry for the word of life. Large additions were made to the Methodist, Presbyterian, and Baptist churches. Mr. Lane's manner of communication was peculiarly calculated to awaken the intellect of the hearer, and arouse the sinner to look about him for safety—much good instruction was always drawn from his discourses on the scriptures, and in common with others, our brother's mind became awakened.

For a length of time the reformation seemed to move in a harmonious manner, but, as the excitement ceased, or those who had expressed anxieties had professed a belief in the pardoning influence and condescension of the Savior, a general struggle was made by the leading characters of the different sects for proselytes. Then strife seemed to take the place of that apparent union and harmony which had previously characterized the moves and exhortations of the old professors, and a cry—"I am right, you are wrong"— was introduced in their stead.

In this general strife for followers, his mother, one sister, and two of his natural brothers were persuaded to unite with the Presbyterians. This gave opportunity for further reflection; and as will be seen in the sequel, laid a foundation, or was one means of laying a foundation for the attestation of the truths, or professions of truth, contained in that record called the word of God.

After strong solicitations to unite with one of those different societies, and seeing the apparent proselyting disposition manifested with equal warmth from each, his mind was led to more seriously contemplate the importance of a move of this kind. To profess godliness without its benign influence upon the heart was a thing so foreign from his feelings that his spirit was not at rest day or night. To unite with a society professing to be built upon the only sure foundation, and that profession be a vain one, was calculated, in its very nature, the more it was contemplated, the more to arouse the mind to the serious consequences of moving hastily, in a course fraught with eternal realities. To say he was right, and still be wrong, could not profit; and amid so many, some must be built upon the sand.

In this situation, where could he go? If he went to one he was told they were right, and all others were wrong. If to another, the same was heard from those: All professed to be the true church; and if not they were certainly hypocritical, because, if I am presented with a system of religion, and inquire of my teacher whether it is correct, and he informs me that he is not certain, he acknowledges at once that he is teaching without authority, and acting without a commission!

If one professed a degree of authority or preference in consequence of age or right, and that superiority was without evidence, it was insufficient to convince a mind once aroused to that degree of determination which at that time operated upon him. And upon further reflecting that the Savior had said that the gate was straight and the way narrow that leads to life eternal, and that few entered there; and that the way was broad, and the gate wide which leads to destruction, and that many crowded its current, a proof from some source was wanting to settle the mind and give peace to the agitated bosom. It is not frequent that the minds of men are exercised with proper determination relative to obtaining a certainty of the things of God. They are too apt to rest short of that assurance which the Lord Jesus has so freely offered in his word to man, and which so beautifully characterizes his whole plan of salvation, as revealed to us.

Letter 4

To W. W. Phelps, Esq.

DEAR BROTHER:

In my last, published in the 3d No. of the *Advocate,* I apologized for the brief manner in which I should be obliged to give, in many instances, the history of this church. Since then yours of Christmas has been received. It was not my wish to be understood that I could not give the leading items of every important occurrence, at least so far as would effect my duty to my fellowmen, in such as contained important information upon the subject of doctrine, and as would render it intelligibly plain; but as there are, in a great house, many vessels, so in the history of a work of this magnitude, many items which would be interesting to those who follow, are forgotten. In fact, I deem every manifestation of the Holy Spirit, dictating the hearts of the saints in the way of righteousness, to be of importance,, and this is one reason why I plead an apology.

You will recollect that I mentioned the time of a religious excitement, in Palmyra and vicinity to have been in the 15th year of our brother J. Smith Jr's, age—that was an error in the type—it should have been in the 17th.[1] You will please remember this correction, as it will be necessary for the full understanding of what will follow in time. This would bring the date down to the year 1823.

I do not deem it to be necessary to write further on the subject of this excitement. It is doubted by many whether any real or essential good ever resulted from such excitements, while others advocate their propriety with warmth.

The mind is easily called up to reflection upon a matter of such deep importance, and it is just that it should be; but there is a regret occupying the heart when we consider the deep anxiety of thousands, who are led away with a vain imagination, or a groundless hope, no better than the idle wind or the spider's web.

But if others were not benefited, our brother was urged forward and strengthened in the determination to know for himself of the certainty and reality of pure and holy religion. And it is only necessary for me to say, that while this excitement continued, he continued to call upon the Lord in secret for a full manifestation of divine approbation, and for, to him, the all important information, if a Supreme being did exist, to have an assurance that he was accepted of him. This, most assuredly, was correct—it was right. The Lord has said, long since, and his word remains steadfast, that for him who knocks it shall be opened, and whosoever will, may come and partake of the waters of life freely.

---

1. This, of course, is incorrect, raising the question of why Oliver felt the need to make this change. One possibility is that he now considered it necessary to exclude any account of Joseph's First Vision, possibly on the advice of the Prophet, who may have felt that the experience was too personal or sacred to include in a newspaper article. Incidentally, "in the 15th year" does not mean "fifteen years old" but rather that Joseph had passed his fourteenth birthday. In other words, he was fourteen years old. For clarification, an infant during its first year of life has not yet reached its first birthday.

To deny a humble penitent sinner a refreshing draught from this most pure of all fountains, and most desirable of all refreshments, to a thirsty soul, is a matter for the full performance of which the sacred record stands pledged. The Lord never said, "Come unto me, all ye that labor, and are heavy laden, and I will give you rest," to turn a deaf ear to those who were weary, when they call upon him. He never said, by the mouth of the prophet, "Ho, every one that thirsts, come ye to the waters," without passing it as a firm decree, at the same time, that he that should after come, should be filled with a joy unspeakable. Neither did he manifest by the Spirit to John upon the isle, "Let him that is athirst, come," and command him to send the same abroad, under any other consideration, than that "whosoever would, might take the water of life freely," to the remotest ages of time, or while there was a sinner upon his footstool.

These sacred and important promises are looked upon in our day as being given, either to another people, or in a figuratively form, and consequently require spiritualizing, notwithstanding they are as conspicuously plain, and are meant to be understood according to their literal reading, as those passages which teach us of the creation of the world, and of the decree of its Maker to bring its inhabitants to judgment. But to proceed with my narrative. On the evening of the 21st of September, 1823, previous to retiring to rest, our brother's mind was unusually wrought up on the subject which had so long agitated his mind—his heart was drawn out in fervent prayer, and his whole soul was so lost to every thing of a temporal nature, that earth, to him, had lost its claims, and all he desired was to be prepared in heart to commune with some kind messenger who could communicate to him the desired information of his acceptance with God.

At length the family retired, and he, as usual, bent his way, though in silence, where others might have rested their weary frames "locked fast in sleep's embrace;" but repose had fled, and accustomed slumber had spread her refreshing hand over others beside him—he continued still to pray—his heart, though once hard and obdurate, was softened, and that mind which had often flitted, like the "wild bird of passage," had settled upon a determined basis not to be decoyed or driven from its purpose.

In this situation hours passed unnumbered—how many or how few I know not, neither is he able to inform me; but supposes it must have been eleven or twelve, and perhaps later, as the noise and bustle of the family, in retiring, had long since ceased. While continuing in prayer for a manifestation in some way that his sins were forgiven; endeavoring to exercise faith in the scriptures, on a sudden a light like that of day, only of a purer and far more glorious appearance and brightness, burst into the room. Indeed, to use his own description, the first sight was as though the house was filled with consuming and unquenchable fire. This sudden appearance of a light so bright, as must naturally be expected, occasioned a shock or sensation, visible to the extremities of the body. It was, however, followed with a calmness and serenity of mind, and an overwhelming rapture of joy that surpassed understanding, and in a moment a personage stood before him.

Notwithstanding the room was previously filled with light above the brightness of the sun, as I have before described, yet there seemed to be an additional glory surrounding or accompanying this personage, which shone with an increased degree of brilliancy, of which he was in the midst; and though his countenance was as lightning, yet it was of a pleasing, innocent and glorious appearance, so much so, that every fear was banished from the heart, and nothing but calmness pervaded the soul.

It is no easy task to describe the appearance of a messenger from the skies—indeed, I doubt there being an individual clothed with perishable clay, who is capable to do this work. To be sure, the Lord appeared to his apostles after his resurrection, and we do not learn as they were in the least difficultied to look upon him; but from John's description upon Patmos, we learn that he is there represented as most glorious in appearance; and from other items in the sacred scriptures we have the fact recorded where angels appeared and conversed with men, and there was no difficulty on the part of the individuals, to endure their presence; and others where their glory was so conspicuous that they could not endure. The last description or appearance is the one to which I refer, when I say that it is no easy task to describe their glory.

But it may be well to relate the particulars as far as given. The stature of this personage was a little above the common size of men in this age; his garment was perfectly white, and had the appearance of being without seam.

Though fear was banished form his heart, yet his surprise was no less when he heard him declare himself to be a messenger sent by commandment of the Lord, to deliver a special message, and to witness to him that his sins were forgiven, and that his prayers were heard; and that the scriptures might be fulfilled, which say, "God has chosen the foolish things of the world to confound the things which are mighty; and base things of the world, and things which are despised, has God chosen; yea, and things which are not, to bring to nought things which are, that no flesh should glory in his presence. Therefore, says the Lord, I will proceed to do a marvelous work among this people, even a marvelous work and a wonder; the wisdom, of their wise shall perish, and the understanding of their prudent shall be hid; for according to his covenant which he made with his ancient saints, his people, the house of Israel, must come to a knowledge of the gospel, and own that Messiah whom their fathers rejected, and with them the fullness of the Gentiles be gathered in, to rejoice in one fold under one Shepherd."

"This cannot be brought about until first certain preparatory things are accomplished, for so has the Lord purposed in his own mind. He has therefore chosen you as an instrument in his hand to bring to light that which shall; perform his act, his strange act, and bring to pass a marvelous work and a wonder. Wherever the sound shall go it shall cause the ears of men to tingle, and wherever it shall be proclaimed, the pure in heart shall rejoice, while those who draw near to God with their mouths, and honor him with their lips, while their hearts are far from him, will seek its overthrow, and the destruction of those by whose hands it is carried. Therefore, marvel not if your name is made a derision, and had as a by-word among such, if you are the instrument in bringing it, by the gift of God, to the knowledge of the people."

He then proceeded and gave a general account of the promises made to the fathers, and also gave a history of the aborigines of this country, and said they were literal descendants of Abraham. He represented them as once being an enlightened and intelligent people, possessing a correct knowledge of the gospel, and the plan of restoration and redemption. He said this history was written and deposited not far from that place, and that it was our brother's privilege, if obedient to the commandments of the Lord, to obtain, and translate the same by the means of the Urim and Thummim, which were deposited for that purpose with the record.

"Yet," said he, "the scripture must be fulfilled before it is translated, which says that the words of a book, which were sealed, were presented to the learned; for thus has God determined to leave men without excuse, and show to the meek that his arm is not shortened that it cannot save." A part of the book was sealed, and was not to be opened yet. The sealed part, said he, contains the same revelation which was given to John upon the isle of Patmos, and when the people of the Lord are prepared, and found worthy, then it will be unfolded unto them.

On the subject of bringing to light the unsealed part of this record, it may be proper to say, that our brother was expressly informed, that it must be done with an eye single to the glory of God; if this consideration did not wholly characterize all his proceedings in relation to it, the adversary of truth would overcome him, or at least prevent his making that proficiency in this glorious work which he otherwise would.

While describing the place where the record was deposited, he gave a minute relation of it, and the vision of his mind being opened at the same time, he was permitted to view it critically; and previously being acquainted with the place, he was able to follow the direction of the vision, afterward, according to the voice of the angel, and obtain the book.

I close for the present by subscribing myself as ever, your brother in Christ.

OLIVER COWDERY.

Kirtland, Ohio, Feb. 27, 1835.

Letter 5

TO W. W. PHELPS, ESQ.

Dear Brother:

Yours of 6th ult. is received and published in this No. It contains so many questions, that I have thought I would let every man answer for himself; as it would occupy a larger space to answer all of them than would be proper to devote at this time. When I look at the world as it is, and view men as they are, I am not much surprised that they oppose the truth as many, perhaps, and indeed, the more I see the less I marvel on this subject. To talk of heavenly communications, angels' visits, and the inspiration of the Holy Spirit, now, since the apostles have fallen asleep, and men interpret the word of God without the aid of either the Spirit or angels, is a novel thing among the wise, and a piece of blasphemy among the craft men. But so it is, and it is wisdom that it should be so, because the Holy Spirit does not dwell in unholy temples, nor angels reveal the great work of God to hypocrites.

You will notice in my last, on rehearsing the words of the angel, where he communicated to our brother—that his sins were forgiven, and that he was called of the Lord to bring to light, by the gift of inspiration, this important intelligence, an item like the following: "God has chosen the foolish things of the world, and things which are despised, God has chosen;" etc. This, I conceive to be an important item. Not many mighty and noble, were called in ancient times, because they always knew so much that God could not teach them, and a man that would listen to the voice of the Lord and follow the teachings of heaven, always was despised, and considered to be of the foolish class. Paul proves this fact, when he says, "We are made as the filth of the world—the off-scouring of all things unto this day."

I am aware, that a rehearsal of visions of angels at this day, is as inconsistent with a portion of mankind as it formerly was, after all the boast of this wise generation in the knowledge of the truth; but there is a uniformity so complete, that on the reflection, one is led to rejoice that it is so.

In my last I gave an imperfect description of the angel, and was obliged to do so, for the reason, that my pen would fail to describe an angel in his glory, or the glory of God. I also gave a few sentences which he uttered on the subject of the gathering of Israel, etc. Since writing the former, I have thought it would, perhaps, be interesting to give something more full on this important subject, as well as a revelation of the gospel. That these holy personages should feel a deep interest in the accomplishment of the glorious purposes of the Lord, in his work in the last days, is consistent, when we view critically what is recorded of their sayings in the holy Scriptures.

You will remember to have read in Daniel "And at that time, [the last days] shall Michael stand up, the great prince, who stands for the children of thy people;" and also in Revelation, "I am thy fellow servant, and of thy brethren the prophets." Please compare these sayings with that singular expression in Heb. "Are they [angels] not all ministering Spirits, sent forth to minister for them who shall be heirs of salvation?" And then let me ask nine questions: first,

Are the angels now in glory, the former prophets and servants of God? Secondly; Are they brethren of those who keep his commandments on earth? and thirdly, have brethren and fleshly kindred, in the kingdom of God, feelings of respect and condescension enough to speak to each other, though one may be in heaven and the other on the earth?

Fourthly: If angels are ministering spirits, sent forth to minister for those who shall be heirs of salvation, will they not minister for those heirs? and fifthly, if they do, will anyone know it?

Sixthly: Will Michael, the archangel, the great prince, stand up in the last days for Israel? Seventhly: will he defend them from their enemies? Eighthly will he lead them, as they were once led; and ninthly, if so, will he be seen? These questions I leave without answering, because the reasoning is so plain, and so many might be brought, that, they must be at hand in the heart and mind of every Saint. But to the gospel, and then to the gathering.

The great plan of redemption being prepared before the fall of man, and the salvation of the human family being as precious in the sight of the Lord at one time as at another, before the Messiah came in the flesh and was crucified, as after the gospel was preached, and many were found obedient to the same. This gospel being the same from the beginning, its ordinances were also unchangeable. Men were commanded to repent and be baptized by water in the name of the Lord: and were then blessed with the Holy Spirit. The Holy Spirit being thus given; men were enabled to look forward to the time of the coming of the Son of Man, and to rejoice in that day, because through that sacrifice they looked for a remission of their sins, and for their redemption.

Had it not been for this plan of salvation, which God devised before the fall, man must have remained miserable forever, after transgressing the first commandment, because in consequence of that transgression he had rendered himself unworthy the presence of his Maker. He being therefore cast out, the gospel was preached, and this hope of eternal life was set before Him, by the ministering of angels who delivered it as they were commanded.

Not only did the ancients look forward to the time of the coming of the Messiah in the flesh, with delight, but there was another day for which they sought and for which they prayed. Knowing, as they did, that the fall had brought upon them death, and that man was sensual and evil, the longed for a day when the earth might again rest, and appear as in the beginning—when evil might be unknown upon its face, and all creation enjoy one undisturbed peace for a thousand years.

This being sought for in faith, it pleased the Lord to covenant with them to roll on his purposes until he should bring it to pass—and though many generations were to be gathered to their fathers, yet the righteous, those who should, in their lives, embrace the gospel, and live obedient to its requirements, rise and inherit it during this reign of peace.

From time to time the faithful servants of the Lord have endeavored to raise up a people who should be found worthy to inherit this rest (for it was called the rest of the righteous or the day of the Lord's rest, prepared for the righteous), but were not able to sanctify them that they could endure the presence of the Lord, excepting Enoch, who, with his people, for their righteousness, were taken into heaven, with a promise that they should yet see that day when the whole earth should be covered with glory.

Moses labored diligently to effect this object, but in consequence of the transgressions and rebellions of the children of Israel, God swore in his wrath that they should not enter into his rest; and in consequence of this decree, and their transgressions since, they have been scattered to the four winds, and are thus to remain till the Lord gathers them in by his own power.

To a remnant of them the gospel was preached by the Messiah in person, but they rejected his voice, though it was raised daily among them. The apostles continued to hold forth the same; after the crucifixion and resurrection of the Lord Jesus until they would bear it no longer; and then they were commanded to turn to the Gentiles.

They however labored faithfully to turn that people from error; that they might be the happy partakers of mercy, and save themselves from the impending storm that hung over them. They were commanded to preach Jesus Christ night and day—to preach through him the resurrection from the dead—to declare that all who would embrace the gospel, repent, and be baptized for the remission of their sins, should be saved—to declare that this was the only sure foundation on which they could build and be safe— that God had again visited his people in consequence of his covenant with their fathers, and that if they would they might be the first who should receive these glad things, and have the unspeakable joy of carrying the same to all people; for before the day of rest comes, it must go to all nations, kindreds and tongues.

But in consequence of their rejecting the gospel, the Lord suffered them to be again scattered; their land to be wasted and their beautiful city to be trodden down of the Gentiles, until their time should be fulfilled.

In the last days, to fulfill the promises to the ancient prophets, when the Lord is to pour out his Spirit upon all flesh, he has determined to bring to light his gospel, to the Gentiles, that it may go to the house of Israel. This gospel has been perverted and men have wandered in darkness. That commission given to the apostles at Jerusalem, so

easy to be understood, has been hid from the world, because of evil, and the honest have been led by the designing, till there are none to be found who are practicing the
ordinances of the gospel, as they were anciently delivered.

But the time has now arrived, in which, according to his
covenants, the Lord will manifest to the faithful that he is
the same to-day and forever, and that the cup of suffering
of his people, the house of Israel, is nearly fulfilled; and that
the way may be prepared before their face he will bring to
the knowledge of the people the gospel as it was preached
by his servants on this land, and manifest to the obedient
the truth of the same, by the power of the Holy Spirit; for
the time is near when his sons and daughters will prophesy,
old men dream dreams, and young men see visions, and
those who are thus favored will be such as embrace the
gospel as it was delivered in old times; and they shall be
blessed with signs following.

Further on the subject of the gathering of Israel: This
was perfectly understood by all the ancient prophets. Moses
prophesied of the affliction which should come upon that
people even after the coming of the Messiah, where he said:
and evil will befall you in the latter days; because ye will
do evil in the sight of the Lord, to provoke him to anger
through the work of your hands. Connecting this with a
prophecy in the song which follows; which was given to
Moses in the tabernacle—remembering the expression—
"in the latter days"—where the Lord foretells all their evil,
and their being received to mercy, to such as seek the peace
of Israel much instruction may be gained. It is as follows:
"I will heap mischiefs upon them; I will spend my arrows
upon them. They shall be burnt with hunger, and devoured
with burning heat: I will also send the teeth of beasts upon
them, with the poison of serpents of the dust. The sword
without, and terror within, shall destroy both the young

man and the virgin, the suckling with the man of gray hairs."

But after all this, he will judge their enemies and avenge them of theirs; for he says:

"If I whet my glittering sword, and my hand take hold on judgment, I will render vengeance to my enemies, and will reward them that hate me. I will make my arrows drunk with blood, and my sword shall devour flesh."

After all this—after Israel has been restored, and afflicted and his enemies have also been chastised, the Lord says: "Rejoice, O ye nations, with his people: for he will avenge the blood of his servants, and will render vengeance to his adversaries, and will be merciful unto his land and to his people."

I will give a further detail of the promises to Israel, hereafter, as rehearsed by the angel. Accept assurance of my esteem as ever.

Letter 6

TO W. W. PHELPS, ESQ.

Dear Sir: Yours of the 24th February is received and inserted in this No. of the *Advocate*. When reviewing my letter No. 3, I am led to conclude, that some expressions contained in it are calculated to call up past scenes, and perhaps, paint them to the mind, in a manner differently than otherwise were it not that you can speak from experience of their correctness.

I have not space you know, to go into every particular item noticed in yours, as that would call my attention too far, or too much, from the great object lying before me—the history of this church—but one expression, or quotation contained in your last strikes the mind (and I may add—the heart) with so much force, that I cannot pass without noticing it: It is a line or two from that little book contained in the Old Testament, called "RUTH." It says: "Entreat me not to leave thee, or to return from following after thee: for whither thou goest, I will go; and where thou lodgest, I will lodge, thy people shall be my people, and thy God my God."

There is a something breathed in this, not known to the world. The great, as many are called, may profess friendship, and covenant to share in each other's toils, for the honors and riches of this life, but it is not like the sacrifice offered by Ruth. She forsook her friends, she left her nation, she longed not for the altars of her former gods, and why? because Israel's God was God indeed? and by joining herself to HIM a reward was offered, and an inheritance promised with him when the earth was sanctified, and peoples, nations and tongues serve him acceptably? And the same covenant of Ruth's, whispers the same assurance in the same promises, and the same knowledge of the same God.

I gave, in my last, a few words, on the subject of a few items, as spoken by the angel at the time the knowledge of the record of the Nephites was communicated to our brother, and in consequence of the subject of the gospel and that of the gathering of Israel's being so connected, I found it difficult to speak of the one without mentioning the other; and this may not be improper, as it is evident, that the Lord has decreed to bring forth the fullness of the gospel in the last days, previous to gathering Jacob, but a preparatory work, and the other is to follow in quick succession.

This being of so much importance, and of so deep interest to the saints, I have thought best to give a further detail of the heavenly message, and if I do not give it in the precise words, shall strictly confine myself to the facts in substance.

David said (Ps. C.), make a joyful noise unto the Lord, all ye lands, that is, all the earth. Serve the Lord with gladness: Come before his presence with singing. This he said in view of the glorious period for which he often prayed, and was anxious to behold, which he knew could not take place until the knowledge of the glory of God covered all lands, or all the earth. Again he says, [Ps. 107] O give thanks unto the Lord, for he is good: For his mercy endureth forever. Let the redeemed of the Lord say so, whom he has redeemed from the hand of the enemy; and gathered out of the lands from the east, and from the west; from the north and from the south. They wandered in the wilderness in a solitary way; they found no city to dwell in. Hungry and thirsty, their soul fainted in them. Then they cried unto the Lord in their trouble, and he delivered them out their distresses; and led them in the right way that they might go to the city of habitation.

Most clearly was it shown to the prophet, that the righteous should be gathered from all the earth: He knew that the children of Israel were led from Egypt, by the right hand of the Lord, and permitted to possess the land of Canaan, though they were rebellious in the desert, but he further knew, that they were not gathered from the east, the west, the north and the south, at that time; for it was clearly manifested that the Lord himself would prepare a habitation, even as he said, when he would lead them to a city of refuge. In that, David saw a promise for the righteous, [see 144 Ps] when they should be delivered from those who oppressed them, and from the hand of strange children, or the enemies of the Lord; that their sons should be like plants grown up in their youth, and their daughters like corner-stones, polished after the similitude of a beautiful palace. It is then that the sons and daughters shall prophesy, old men dream dreams, and young men see visions. At that time the garners of the righteous will be full, affording all manner of store. It was while contemplating this time, and viewing this happy state of the righteous, that he further says: The Lord shall reign forever, even thy God, O Zion, unto all generations—Praise ye the Lord!

Isaiah who was on the earth at the time the ten tribes of Israel were led away captive from the land of Canaan, was shown, not only their calamity and affliction, but the time when they were to be delivered. After reproving them for their corruption and blindness, he prophesies of their dispersion. He says, Your country is desolate, your cities are burnt with fire: Your land, strangers devour it in your presence, and it is thus made desolate, being overthrown by strangers. He further says, while speaking of the iniquity of that people. Thy princes are rebellious, and companions of thieves: every one loves gifts, and follows after rewards: They judge not the fatherless, neither does the cause of the widow come unto them. Therefore, says the Lord, the Lord of hosts, the mighty One of Israel, Ah, I will ease me of my adversaries, and avenge me of my enemies. But after this calamity has befallen Israel, and the Lord has poured upon them his afflicting judgments, as he said by the mouth of Moses—I will heap mischiefs upon them; I will spend my arrows upon them. They shall be afflicted with hunger, and devoured with burning heat, and with bitter destruction: I will also send the teeth of beasts upon them, with the poison of serpents of the earth—he will also fulfill this further prediction uttered by the mouth of Isaiah. I will turn my hand upon thee, and purely purge away thy dross, and take away all thy tin: and I will restore thy judges as at the first, and thy counsellors as at the beginning: afterward you shall be called, the city of righteousness, the faithful city. Then will be fulfilled, also, the saying of David: And he led them forth by the right way, that they might go to a city of habitation.

Isaiah continues his prophecy concerning Israel, and tells them what would be done for them in the last days; for thus it is written: The word that Isaiah the son of Amos saw concerning Judah and Jerusalem. And it shall come to pass in the last days, that the mountain of the Lord's house shall be established in the top of the mountains, and shall be exalted above the hills; and all nations shall flow unto it. And many people shall go and say, Come ye, and let us go up to the mountain of the Lord, to the house of the God of Jacob; and he will teach us of his ways and we will walk in his paths: for out of Zion shall go forth the law, and the word of the Lord from Jerusalem. And he shall judge among the nations, and shall rebuke many people: and they shall beat their swords into plough shares, and their spears into pruning hooks: nations shall not lift up the sword against nation, neither shall they learn war any more. And the Lord will create upon every dwelling place of his people in Zion, and upon their assemblies, a cloud and smoke by day, and the shining of a flaming fire by night: for upon all the glory shall be a defence or above, shall be a covering and a defence. And there shall be a tabernacle for a shadow in the day-time from the heat, and for a place of refuge, and for a covert from storm and from rain. And his people shall dwell safely, they shall possess the land forever, even the land which was promised to their fathers for an everlasting inheritance: for behold, says the Lord by the mouth of the prophet: The day will come that I will sow the house of Israel with the seed of man, and with the seed of beast. And it shall come to pass, that like as I have watched over them, to pluck up, and to break down, and to throw down, and to destroy, and to afflict; so will I watch over them, to build and to plant, says the Lord.

For this happy situation and blessed state of Israel, did the prophets look, and obtained a promise, that, though the house of Israel and Judah, should violate the covenant, the Lord, in the last days would make with them a new one: not according to the one which he made with their fathers in the day that he took them by the hand to lead them out of the land of Egypt; which, said the Lord, my covenant they broke, although I was a husband and a father unto them: but this shall be the covenant that I will make with the house of Israel: After those days, says the Lord. I will put my law in their inward parts, and will write it in their hearts; and I will be their God, and they shall be my people.

For thus says the Lord, I will bring again the captivity of Jacob's tents, and have mercy on his dwelling places; and the city shall be builded upon her own heap, and the palace shall remain after the manner thereof. And out of them shall proceed thanksgiving, and the voice of them that make merry: and I will multiply them and they shall not be few; I will also glorify them and they shall not be small. Their children also shall be as aforetime, and their congregation shall be established before me, and I will punish all that oppress them. Their nobles shall be of themselves, and their governor shall proceed from the midst of them.

At the same time, says the Lord, will I be the God of all the families of Israel, and they shall be my people; I will bring them from the north country, and gather them from the coasts of the earth; I will say to the north, Give up, and to the south, keep not back: bring my sons from far, and my daughters from the ends of the earth. And in those days, and at that time, says the Lord, though Israel and Judah have been driven and scattered, they shall come together, they shall even come weeping: for with supplications will I lead them: they shall go and seek the Lord their God. They shall ask the way to Zion, with their faces thitherward, and say, Come, and let us join ourselves to the Lord in a perpetual covenant that shall not be forgotten; and watchmen upon Mount Ephraim shall say, Arise, and let us go up to Zion, unto the holy Mount of the Lord our God; for he will teach us of his ways, and instruct us to walk in his paths. That the way for this to be fully accomplished, may be prepared, the Lord will utterly destroy the tongue of the Egyptian sea, and with his mighty wind shake his hand over the river and smite it in its seven streams, and make men go over dry-shod. And there shall be a high way for the remnant of his people, which shall be left, from Assyria; like as it was to Israel when they came up out of the land of Egypt.

And thus shall Israel come: not a dark corner of the earth shall remain unexplored, nor an island of the seas be left without being visited; for as the Lord has removed them into all corners of the earth, he will cause his mercy to be as abundantly manifested in their gathering as his wrath in their dispersion, until they are gathered according to the covenant. He will, as he said by the prophet, send for many fishers and they shall fish them; and after send for many hunters, who shall hunt them; not as their enemies have to afflict, but with glad tidings of great joy, with a message of peace, and a call for their return.

And it will come to pass, that though the house of Israel has forsaken the Lord, and bowed down and worshipping other gods, which were no gods, and been cast out before the face of the world, they will know the voice of the Shepherd when he calls upon them this time; for soon his day of power comes, and in it his people will be willing to harken to his counsel; and even now are they already beginning to be stirred up in their hearts to search for these things, and are daily reading the ancient prophets, and are marking the times, and seasons of their fulfillment. Thus God is preparing the way for their return.

But it is necessary that you should understand, that what is to be fulfilled in the last days, Is not only for the benefit of Israel, but the Gentiles, if they will repent and embrace the gospel, for they are to be remembered also in the same covenant, and are to be fellow heirs with the seed of Abraham, inasmuch as they are so by faith—for God is no respecter of persons. This was shown to Moses, when he wrote—Rejoice, O ye nations, with his people!

In consequence of the transgression of the Jews at the coming of the Lord, the Gentiles were called into the kingdom, and for this obedience, are to be favored with the gospel in its fullness first, in the last days; for it is written. The first shall be last, and the last first. Therefore, when the fullness of the gospel, as was preached by the righteous, upon this land, shall come forth, it shall be declared to the Gentiles first, and whoso will repent shall be delivered, for they shall understand the plan of salvation and restoration for Israel, as the Lord manifested to the ancients. They shall be baptized with water and with the Spirit—they shall lift up their hearts with joy and gladness, for the time of their redemption shall also roll on, and for their obedience to the faith they shall see the house of Jacob come with great glory, even with songs of everlasting joy, and with him partake of salvation.

Therefore, as the time draws near when the sun is to be darkened, the moon turn to blood, and the stars fall from heaven, the Lord will bring to the knowledge of his people his commandments and statutes, that they may be prepared to stand when the earth shall reel to and fro as a drunken man, earthquakes cause the nations to tremble, and the destroying angel goes forth to waste the inhabitants at noon-day: for so great are to be the calamities which are to come upon the inhabitants of the earth, before the coming of the Son of Man the second time, that whoso is not prepared cannot abide; but such as are found faithful, and remain, shall be gathered with his people and caught up to meet the Lord in the cloud, and so shall they inherit eternal life.

I have now given you a rehearsal of what was communicated to our brother, when he was directed to go and obtain the record of the Nephites. I may have missed in arrangement in some instances, but the principle is preserved, and you will be able to bring forward abundance of corroborating scripture upon the subject of the gospel and of the gathering. You are aware of the fact, that to give a minute rehearsal of a lengthy interview with a heavenly messenger, is very difficult, unless one is assisted immediately with the gift of inspiration. There is another item I wish to notice on the subject of visions. The Spirit you know, searches all things, even the deep things of God. When God manifests to his servants those things that are to come, or those which have been, he does it by unfolding them by the power of that Spirit which comprehends all things, always; and so much may be shown and made perfectly plain to the understanding in a short time, that to the world, who are occupied all their life to learn a little, look at the relation of it, and are disposed to call it false. You will understand then, by this, that while those glorious things were being rehearsed, the vision was also opened, so that our brother was permitted to see and understand much more full and perfect than I am able to communicate in writing. I know much may be conveyed to the understanding in writing, and many marvelous truths set forth with the pen, but after all it is but a shadow, compared to an open vision of seeing, hearing and realizing eternal things. And if the fact was known, it would be found, that of all the heavenly communications to the ancients, we have no more in comparison than the alphabet to a quarto vocabulary. It is said, and I believe the account, that the Lord showed the brother of Jared all things which were to transpire from that day to the end of the earth, as well as those which had taken place. I believe that Moses was permitted to see the same, as the Lord caused them to pass, in vision before him as he stood upon the mount; I believe that the Lord Jesus told many things to his apostles which are not written, and after his ascension unfolded all things unto them; I believe that Nephi, the son of Lehi, whom the

Lord brought out of Jerusalem, saw the same; I believe that the twelve upon this continent, whom the Lord chose to preach his gospel, when he came down to manifest to this branch of the house of Israel, that he had other sheep who should hear his voice, were also permitted to behold the same mighty things transpire in vision before their eyes; and I believe that the angel Moroni, whose words I have been rehearsing, who communicated the knowledge of the record of the Nephites, in this age, saw also, before he hid up the same unto the Lord, great and marvelous things, which were to transpire when the same should come forth; and I also believe, that God will give line upon line, precept upon precept, to his saints, until all these things will be unfolded to them, and they finally sanctified and brought into the Celestial glory, where tears will be wiped from all faces, and sighing and sorrowing flee away!

May the Lord preserve you from evil and reward you richly for all your afflictions, and crown you in his kingdom. Amen.

Accept, as ever, assurances of the fellowship and esteem of your unworthy brother in the gospel.

Letter 7

TO W. W. Phelps, ESQ.

DEAR BROTHER: Circumstances having heretofore intervened to prevent my addressing you previously upon the history of this church, you will not attribute the neglect to any want on my part, of a disposition to prosecute a subject so dear to me and so important to every saint, living as we do in the day when the Lord has began to fulfill his covenants to his long-dispersed and afflicted people.

Since my last yours of May and June have been received. It will not be expected that I shall digress so far from my object, as to go into particular explanations on different items contained in yours; but as all men are deeply interested on the great matter of revelation, I indulge a hope that you will present such facts as are plain and incontrovertible, both from our former scriptures and the book of Mormon, to show that such is not only consistent with the character of the Lord, but absolutely necessary to the fulfillment of that sacred volume, so tenaciously admired by professors of religion—I mean that called the bible.

You have, no doubt, as well as myself, frequently heard those who do not pretend to an "experimental" belief in the Lord Jesus, say, with those who do, that (to use a familiar phrase) "any tune can be played upon the bible:" What is here meant to be conveyed, I suppose, is, that proof can be adduced from that volume, to support as many different systems as men please to choose: one saying this is the way, and the other, this is the way, while the third says, that it is all false, and that he can "play this tune upon it." If this is so, alas for our condition: admit this to be the case, and either wicked and designing men have taken from it those plain and easy items, or it never came from Deity, if that Being is perfect and consistent in his ways.

But although I am ready to admit that men, in previous generations, have, with polluted hands and corrupt hearts, taken from the sacred oracles many precious items which were plain of comprehension, for the main purpose of building themselves up in the trifling things of this world, yet, when it is carefully examined, a straightforward consistency will be found, sufficient to check the vicious heart of man and teach him to revere a word so precious, handed down to us from our fathers, teaching us that by faith we can approach the same benevolent Being, and receive for ourselves a sure word of prophecy, which will serve as a light in a dark place, to lead to those things within the veil, where peace, righteousness and harmony, in one uninterrupted round, feast the inhabitants of those blissful regions in endless day.

Scarce can the reflecting mind be brought to contemplate these scenes, without asking, for whom are they held in reserve, and by whom are they to be enjoyed? Have we an interest there? Do our fathers, who have waded through affliction and adversity, who have been cast out from the society of this world, whose tears have, times without number, watered their furrowed face, while mourning over the corruption of their fellowmen, an inheritance in those mansions? If so, can they without us be made perfect? Will their joy be full till we rest with them? And is their efficacy and virtue sufficient, in the blood of a Savior, who groaned upon Calvary's summit, to expiate our sins and cleanse us from all unrighteousness? I trust, that as individuals acquainted with the gospel, through repentance, baptism and keeping the commandments of that same Lord, we shall eventually, be brought to partake in the fullness of that which we now only participate—the full enjoyment of the presence of our Lord. Happy indeed, will be that hour to all the saints, and above all to be desired (for it never ends), when men will again mingle praise with those who do always behold the face of our Father who is in heaven.

You will remember that in my last I brought my subject down to the evening, or night of the 21st of September, 1823, and gave an outline of the conversation of the angel upon the important fact of the blessings, promises and covenants to Israel, and the great manifestations of favor to the world, in the ushering in of the fullness of the gospel, to prepare the way for the second advent of the Messiah, when he comes in the glory of the Father with the holy angels.

A remarkable fact is to be noticed with regard to this vision. In ancient time the Lord warned some of his servants in dreams: for instance, Joseph, the husband of Mary, was warned in a dream to take the young child and his mother, and flee into Egypt: also, the wise men were warned of the Lord in a dream not to return to Herod; and when "out of Egypt the Son was called," the angel of the Lord appeared in a dream to Joseph again: also he was warned in a dream to turn aside into the parts of Galilee. Such were the manifestations to Joseph, the favored descendant of the father of the faithful in dreams, and in them the Lord fulfilled his purposes: But the tone of which I have been speaking is what would have been called an open vision. And though it was in the night, yet it was not a dream.

There is no room for conjecture in this matter, and to talk of deception would be to sport with the common sense of every man who knows when he is awake, when he sees and when he does not see.

He could not have been deceived in the fact that a being of some kind appeared to him; and that it was an heavenly one, the fulfillment of his words, so minutely, up to this time, in addition to the truth and word of salvation which has been developed to this generation, in the Book of Mormon, ought to be conclusive evidence to the mind of every man who is privileged to hear of the same. He was awake, and in solemn prayer, as you will bear in mind, when the angel made his appearance; from that glory which surrounded him the room was lit up to a perfect brilliancy, so that darkness wholly disappeared: he heard his words with his ears, and received a joy and happiness indescribable by hearing that his own sins were forgiven, and his former transgressions to be remembered against him no more, if he then continued to walk before the Lord according to his holy commandments. He also saw him depart, the light and glory withdraw, leaving a calmness and peace of soul past the language of man to paint. Was he deceived?

Far from this; for the vision was renewed twice before morning, unfolding further and still further the mysteries of godliness and those things to come. In the morning he went to his labor as usual, but soon the vision of the heavenly messenger was renewed, instructing him to go immediately and view those things of which he had been informed, with a promise that he should obtain them if he followed the directions and went with an eye single to the glory of God.

Accordingly he repaired to the place which had thus been described. But it is necessary to give you more fully the express instructions of the angel, with regard to the object of this work in which our brother had now engaged. He was to remember that it was the work of the Lord, to fulfill certain promises previously made to a branch of the house of Israel, of the tribe of Joseph, and when it should be brought forth must be done expressly with an eye, as I said before, single to the glory of God, and the welfare and restoration of the house of Israel.

You will understand, then, that no motive of a pecuniary, or earthly nature, was to be suffered to take the lead of the heart of the man thus favored. The allurements of vice, the contaminating influence of wealth, without the direct guidance of the Holy Spirit, must have no place in the heart nor be suffered to take from it that warm desire for the glory and kingdom of the Lord, or, instead of obtaining, disappointment and reproof would most assuredly follow. Such was the instruction and this the caution.

Alternately, as we could naturally expect, the thought of the previous vision was ruminating in his mind, with a reflection of the brightness and glory of the heavenly messenger; but again a thought would start across the mind on the prospects of obtaining so desirable a treasure—one in all human probability sufficient to raise him above a level with the common earthly fortunes of his fellow men, and relieve his family from want, in which, by misfortune and sickness they were placed.

It is very natural to suppose that the mind would revolve upon those scenes which had passed, when those who had acquired a little of this world's goods, by industry and economy, with the blessings of health or friends, or by art and intrigue, from the pockets of the day-laborer, or the widow and the fatherless, had passed by with a stiff neck and a cold heart, scorning the virtuous because they were poor, and lording over those who were subjected to suffer the miseries of this life.

Alternately did these, with a swift reflection of the words of the holy messenger, "Remember, that he who does this work, who is thus favored of the Lord, must do it with his eye single to the glory of the same, and the welfare and restoration of the scattered remnants of the house of Israel"—rush upon his mind with the quickness of electricity. Here was a struggle indeed; for when he calmly reflected upon his errand, he knew that if God did not give, he could not obtain; and again, with the thought or hope of obtaining, his mind would be carried back to its former reflection of poverty, abuse—wealth, grandeur and ease, until before arriving at the place described, this wholly occupied his desire; and when he thought upon the fact of what was previously shown him, it was only with an assurance that he should obtain, and accomplish his desire in relieving himself and friends from want.

A history of the inhabitants who peopled this continent, previous to its being discovered to Europeans by Columbus, must be interesting to every man; and as it would develop the important fact, that the present race were descendants of Abraham, and were to be remembered in the immutable covenant of the Most High to that man, and be restored to a knowledge of the gospel, that they, with all nations might rejoice, seemed to inspire further thoughts of gain and income from such a valuable history. Surely, thought he, every man will seize with eagerness, this knowledge, and this incalculable income will be mine. Enough to raise the expectations of anyone of like inexperience, placed in similar circumstances. But the important point in this matter is, that man does not see as the Lord, neither are his purposes like his. The small things of this life are but dust in comparison with salvation and eternal life.

It is sufficient to say that such were his reflections during his walk of from two to three miles: the distance from his father's house to the place pointed out. And to use his own words it seemed as though two invisible powers were influencing, or striving to influence his mind—one with the reflection that if he obtained the object of his pursuit, it would be through the mercy and condescension of the Lord, and that every act or performance in relation to it, must be in strict accordance with the instruction of that personage who communicated the intelligence to him first; and the other with the thoughts and reflections like those previously mentioned—contrasting his former and present circumstances in life with those to come. That precious instructions recorded on the sacred page—pray always—which was expressly impressed upon him, was at length entirely forgotten, and as I previously remarked, a fixed determination to obtain and aggrandize himself, occupied his mind when he arrived at the place where the record was found.

I must now give you some description of the place where, and the manner in which these records were deposited.

You are acquainted with the mail road from Palmyra, Wayne Co. to Canandaigua, Ontario Co. N. Y. and also, as you pass from the former to the latter place, before arriving at the little village of Manchester, say from three to four, or about four miles from Palmyra, you pass a large hill on the east side of the road. Why I say large, is, because it is as large perhaps, as any in that country. To a person acquainted with this road, a description would be unnecessary, as it is the largest and rises the highest of any on that route. The north end rises quite sudden until it assumes a level with the more southerly extremity, and I think I may say an elevation higher than at the south a short distance, say half or three fourths of a mile. As you pass toward Canandaigua it lessens gradually until the surface assumes its common level, or is broken by other smaller hills or ridges, water courses and ravines. I think I am justified in saying that this is the highest hill for some distance round, and I am certain that its appearance, as it rises so suddenly from a plain on the north, must attract the notice of the traveler as he passes by.

At about one mile west rises another ridge of less height, running parallel with the former, leaving a beautiful vale between. The soil is of the first quality for the country, and under a state of cultivation, which gives a prospect at once imposing, when one reflects on the fact, that here, between these hills, the entire power and national strength of both the Jaredites and Nephites were destroyed.

By turning to the 529th and 530th pages of the Book of Mormon you will read Mormon's account of the last great struggle of his people, as they were encamped round this hill Cumorah. (It is printed Camorah, which is an error.) In this valley fell the remaining strength and pride of a once powerful people, the Nephites—once so highly favored of the Lord, but at that time in darkness, doomed to suffer extermination by the hand of their barbarous and uncivilized brethren. From the top of this hill, Mormon, with a few others, after the battle, gazed with horror upon the mangled remains of those who, the day before, were filled with anxiety, hope, or doubt. A few had fled to the South, who were hunted down by the victorious party, and all who would not deny the Savior and his religion, were put to death. Mormon himself, according to the record of his son Moroni, was also slain.

But a long time previous to this national disaster, it appears from his own account, he foresaw approaching destruction. In fact, if he perused the records of his fathers, which were in his possession, he could have learned that such would be the case. Alma, who lived before the coming of the Messiah, prophesies this. He however, by divine appointment, abridged from those records, in his own style and language, a short account of the more important and prominent items, from the days of Lehi to his own time, after which he deposited, as he says, on the 529th page, all the records in this same hill, Cumorah, and after gave his small record to his son Moroni, who, as appears from the same, finished, after witnessing the extinction of his people as a nation.

It was not the wicked who overcame the righteous; far from this: it was the wicked against the wicked, and by the wicked the wicked were punished. The Nephites who were once enlightened, had fallen from a more elevated standing as to favor and privilege before the Lord, in consequence of the righteousness of their fathers, and now falling below, for such was actually the case, were suffered to be overcome, and the land was left to the possession of the red men, who were without intelligence, only in the affairs of their wars; and having no records, only preserving their history by tradition from father to son, lost the account of their true origin, and wandered from river to river, from hill to hill, from mountain to mountain, and from sea to sea, till the land was again peopled, in a measure, by a rude, wild, revengeful, warlike and barbarous race. Such are our Indians.

This hill, by the Jaredites, was called Ramah: by it, or around it, pitched the famous army of Coriantumr their tents. Coriantumr was the last king of the Jaredites. The opposing army were to the west, and in this same valley, and near by, from day to day, did that mighty race spill their blood, in wrath, contending, as it were, brother against brother, and father, against son. In this same spot, in full view from the top of this same hill, one may gaze with astonishment upon the ground which was twice covered with the dead and dying of our fellowmen. Here may be seen where once sunk to nought the pride and strength of two mighty nations; and here may be contemplated, in solitude, while nothing but the faithful record of Mormon and Moroni is now extant to inform us of the fact, scenes of misery and distress—the aged, whose silver locks in other places and at other times would command reverence; the mother, who in other circumstances would be spared from violence; the infant, whose tender cries would be regarded and listened to with a feeling of compassion and tenderness; and the virgin, whose grace, beauty and modesty, would be esteemed and held inviolate by all good men and enlightened and civilized nations, alike disregarded and treated with scorn! In vain did the hoary head and man of gray hairs ask for mercy; in vain did the mother plead for compassion; in vain did the helpless and harmless infant weep for very anguish, and in vain did the virgin seek to escape the ruthless hand of revengeful foes and demons in human form—all alike were trampled down by the feet of the strong, and crushed beneath the rage of battle and war! Alas, who can reflect upon the last struggles of great and populous nations, sinking to dust beneath the hand of justice and retribution, without weeping over the corruption of the human heart, and sighing for the hour when the clangor of arms shall no more be heard, nor the calamities of contending armies no more experienced for a thousand years? Alas, the calamity of war, the extinction of nations, the ruin of kingdoms, the fall of empires and the dissolution of governments! O the misery, distress and evil attendant on these! Who can contemplate like scenes without sorrowing, and who so destitute of commiseration as not to be pained that man has fallen so low, so far beneath the station in which he was created?

In this vale lie commingled, in one mass of ruin, the ashes of thousands, and in this vale was destined to consume the fair forms and vigorous systems of tens of thousands of the human race—blood mixed with blood, flesh with flesh, bones with bones, and dust with dust! When the vital spark which animated their clay had fled, each lifeless lump lay on one common level—cold and inanimate. Those bosoms which had burned with rage against each other for real or supposed injury, had now ceased to heave with malice; those arms which were, a few moments before nerved with strength, had alike become paralyzed, and those hearts which had been fired with revenge, had now ceased to heave with malice; those arms which were, a few moments before nerved with strength, had alike become paralyzed, and those hearts which had been fired with revenge, had now ceased to beat, and the head to think— in silence, in solitude, and in disgrace alike, they have long since turned to earth, to their mother dust, to await the august, and to millions, awful hour, when the trump of the Son of God shall echo and re-echo from the skies, and they come forth, quickened and immortalized, to not only stand in each other's presence, but before the bar of him who is Eternal!

With sentiments of pure respect, I conclude by subscribing myself your brother in the gospel.

OLIVER COWDERY.

Letter 8

Dear Brother,

In my last I said I should give, partially, a "description of the place where, and the manner in which these records were deposited": the first promise I have fulfilled, and must proceed to the latter.

The hill of which I have been speaking, at the time mentioned, presented a varied appearance: the north end rose suddenly from the plain, forming a promontory without timber, but covered with grass. As you passed to the south, you soon came to scattering timber, the surface having been cleared by art [human workmanship] or by wind; and a short distance further left, you are surrounded with the common forest of the country. It is necessary to observe that even the part cleared was only occupied for pasturage, its steep ascent and narrow summit not admitting the plow of the husbandman with any degree of ease or profit. It was at the second mentioned place where the record was found to be deposited, on the west side of the hill, not far from the top down its side; and when myself visited the place in the year 1830, there were several trees standing: enough to cause a shade in summer, but not so much as to prevent the surface being covered with grass—which was also the case when the record was first found.

Whatever may be the feeling of men on the reflection of past acts which have been performed on certain portions or spots of this earth, I know not, neither does it add or diminish to nor from the reality of my subject. When Moses heard the voice of God, at the foot of Horeb, out of the burning bush, he was commanded to take his shoes off his feet, for the ground on which he stood was holy. The same may be observed when Joshua beheld the "Captain of the Lord's host" by Jericho. And I confess that my mind was filled with many reflections; and though I did not then loose my shoe, yet with gratitude to God did I offer up the sacrifice of my heart.

How far below the surface these records were placed by Moroni, I am unable to say; but from the fact that they had been some fourteen hundred years buried, and that too on the side of a hill so steep, one is ready to conclude that they were some feet below, as the earth would naturally wear more or less in that length of time, but they being placed toward the top of the hill, the ground would not remove as much as at two-thirds, perhaps. Another circumstance would prevent a wearing of the earth: in all probability, as soon as timber had time to grow, the hill was covered, after the Nephites were destroyed, and the roots of the same would hold the surface. However, on this point I shall leave every man to draw his own conclusion, and form his own speculation, as I only promised to give a description of the place at the time the records were found in 1823. It is sufficient for my present purpose to know that such is the fact: that in 1823, yes, 1823, a man with whom I have had the most intimate and personal acquaintance for almost seven years actually discovered by the vision of God the plates from which the Book of Mormon, as much as it is disbelieved, was translated! Such is the case, though men rack their very brains to invent falsehoods, and then waft them upon every breeze, to the contrary notwithstanding.

I have now given sufficient on the subject of the hill Cumorah—it has a singular and imposing appearance for that country, and must excite the curious inquiry of every lover of the Book of Mormon: though I hope never like Jerusalem, and the sepulcher of our Lord, the pilgrims. In my estimation, certain places are dearer to me for what they now contain than for what they have contained.[1] For the satisfaction of such as believed I have been thus particular, and to avoid the question being a thousand times asked, more than any other cause, shall proceed and be as particular as heretofore. The manner in which the plates were deposited:

First, a hole of sufficient depth (how deep I know not) was dug. At the bottom of this was laid a stone of suitable size, the upper surface being smooth. At each edge was placed a large quantity of cement, and into this cement, at the four edges of this stone, were placed, erect, four others, their bottom edges resting in the cement at the outer edges of the first stone. The four last named, when placed erect, formed a box; the corners, or where the edges of the four came in contact, were also cemented so firmly that the moisture from without was prevented from entering. It is to be observed, also, that the inner surface of the four erect or side stones was smooth. This box was sufficiently large to admit a breast-plate, such as was used by the ancients to defend the chest, etc., from the arrows and weapons of their enemy. From the bottom of the box, or from the breast-plate, arose three small pillars composed of the same description of cement used on the edges; and upon

---

1. This cryptic remark may find an explanation in a story related by Brigham Young in which Oliver and Joseph entered a cave in the Hill Cumorah where they deposited the gold plates after the translation was finished. In this cave were piles of other plates and other sacred artifacts. (*Journal of Discourses*, 19:38.)

these three pillars was placed the record of the children of Joseph, and of a people who left the tower far, far before the days of Joseph, or a sketch of each, which had it not been for this, and the never-failing goodness of God, we might have perished in our sins, having been left to bow down before the altars of the Gentiles and to have paid homage to the priests of Baal!

I must not forget to say that this box containing the record was covered with another stone, the bottom surface being flat and the upper, crowning. But those three pillars were not so lengthy as to cause the plates and the crowning stone to come in contact.[2] I have now given you, according to my promise, the manner in which this record was deposited; though when it was first visited by our brother, in 1823, a part of the crowning stone was visible above the surface while the edges were concealed by the soil and grass, from which circumstance you will see that however deep this box might have been placed by Moroni at first, the time had been sufficient to wear the earth so that it was easily discovered, when once directed, and yet not enough to make a perceivable difference to the passer by. So wonderful are the works of the Almighty, and so far from our finding out are his ways, that one who trembles to take his holy name into his lips is left to wonder at his exact providences, and the fulfilment of his purposes in the event of times and seasons. A few years sooner might have found even the top stone concealed, and discouraged our brother

---

2. In 1875 David Whitmer told a newspaper reporter that "three times has he been at the hill Cumorah and seen the casket that contained the tablets and the seer-stone. Eventually the casket had been washed down to the foot of the hill, but it was to be seen when he last visited the historic place." (*Chicago Times,* August 7, 1875, in Lyndon W. Cook, ed., *David Whitmer Interviews: A Restoration Witness* (Orem, Utah: Grandin, 1991), 7.

from attempting to make a further trial to obtain this rich treasure, for fear of discovery; and a few later might have left the small box uncovered, and exposed its valuable contents to the rude calculations and vain speculations of those who neither understand common language nor fear God, but such would have been contrary to the words of the ancients and the promises made to them: and this is why I am left to admire the words and see the wisdom in the designs of the Lord in all things manifested to the eyes of the world: they who show that all human inventions are like the vapors, while his word endures forever and his promises to the last generation.

Having thus digressed from my main subject to give a few items for the special benefit of all, it will be necessary to return, and proceed as formerly. And if any suppose I have indulged too freely in reflections, I will only say that it is my opinion, were one to have a view of the glory of God which is to cover Israel in the last days, and know that these, though they may be thought small things, were the beginning to effect the same, they would be at a loss where to close, should they give a moment's vent to the imaginations of the heart.

You will have wondered, perhaps, that the mind of our brother should be so occupied with the thoughts of the good of this world, at the time of arriving at Cumorah, on the morning of the 22nd of September, 1823, after having been rapt in the visions of heaven during the night, and also seeing and hearing in open day; but the mind of man is easily turned, if it is not held by the power of God through the prayer of faith, and you will remember that I have said that two invisible powers were operating upon his mind during his walk from his residence to Cumorah, and that the one urging the certainty of wealth and ease in this life had so powerfully wrought upon him, that the great object so carefully and impressively named by the angel had entirely gone from his recollection, that only a fixed determination to obtain now urged him forward. In this, which occasioned a failure to obtain, at that time, the record, do not understand me to attach blame to our brother: he was young, and his mind easily turned from correct principles, unless he could be favored with a certain round of experience. And yet, while young, untraditionated, and untaught in the systems of the world, he was in a situation to be led into the great work of God, and be qualified to perform it in due time.

After arriving at the repository, a little exertion in removing the soil from the edges of the top of the box, and a light pry, brought to his natural vision its contents. No sooner did he behold this sacred treasure than his hopes were renewed, and he supposed his success certain; and without first attempting to take it from its long place of deposit, he thought, perhaps, there might be something more equally as valuable, and to take only the plates might give others an opportunity of obtaining the remainder, which could he secure, would still add to his store of wealth. These, in short, were his reflections, without once thinking of the solemn instruction of the heavenly messenger that all must be done with an express view of glorying God.

On attempting to take possession of the record, a shock was produced upon his system, by an invisible power which deprived him, in a measure, of his natural strength. He desisted for an instant, and then made another attempt, but was more sensibly shocked than before. What was the occasion of this he knew not—there was the pure unsullied record, as had been described—he had heard of the power of enchantment, and a thousand like stories, which held the hidden treasures of the earth, and supposed that physical exertion and personal strength was only necessary to enable him to yet obtain the object of his wish. He therefore made the third attempt with an increased exertion, when his strength failed him more than at either of the former times, and without premeditating he exclaimed, "Why can I not obtain this book?" "Because you have not kept the commandments of the Lord," answered a voice, within a seeming short distance. He looked, and to his astonishment, there stood the angel who had previously given him the directions concerning this matter. In an instant, all the former instructions, the great intelligence concerning Israel and the last days, were brought to his mind: he thought of the time when his heart was fervently engaged in prayer to the Lord, when his spirit was contrite, and when his holy messenger from the skies unfolded the wonderful things connected with this record. He had come, to be sure, and found the word of the angel fulfilled concerning the reality of the record, but he had failed to remember the great end for which they had been kept, and in consequence could not have power to take them into his possession and bear them away.

At that instant he looked to the Lord in prayer, and as he prayed, darkness began to disperse from his mind and his soul was lit up as it was the evening before, and he was filled with the Holy Spirit; and again did the Lord manifest his condescension and mercy: the heavens were opened and the glory of the Lord shone round about and rested upon him. While he thus stood gazing and admiring, the angel said, "Look!" and as he thus spake he beheld the prince of darkness, surrounded by his innumerable train of associates. All this passed before him, and the heavenly messenger said, "All this is shown, the good and the evil, the holy and impure, the glory of God and the power of darkness, that you may know hereafter the two powers and never be influenced or overcome by that wicked one.

Behold, whatever entices and leads to good and to do good, is of God, and whatever does not is of that wicked one:[3] It is he that fills the hearts of men with evil, to walk in darkness and blaspheme God; and you may learn from henceforth, that his ways are to destruction, but the way of holiness is peace and rest.

"You now see why you could not obtain this record; that the commandment was strict, and that if ever these sacred things are obtained they must be by prayer and faithfulness in obeying the Lord. They are not deposited here for the sake of accumulating gain and wealth for the glory of this world: they were sealed by the prayer of faith, and because of the knowledge which they contain they are of no worth among the children of men, only for their knowledge. On them is contained the fullness of the gospel of Jesus Christ, as it was given to his people on this land, and when it shall be brought forth by the power of God, it shall be carried to the Gentiles, of whom many will receive it, and after will the seed of Israel be brought into the fold of their Redeemer by obeying it also.

"Those who keep the commandments of the Lord on this land desired this at his hand, and through the prayer of faith obtained the promises that if their descendants should transgress and fall away, that a record might be kept and in the last days come to their children. These things are sacred, and must be kept so, for the promise of the Lord concerning them must be fulfilled. No man can obtain them if his heart is impure, because they contain that which is sacred; and besides, should they be entrusted in unholy hands, the knowledge could not come to the world, because they cannot be interpreted by the learning

---

3. Moroni taught this same principle in his record in the Book of Mormon (see Moroni 7:13–17).

of this generation; consequently, they would be considered of no worth, only as precious metal.

"Therefore, remember, that they are to be translated by the gift and power of God. By them will the Lord work a great and a marvelous work: the wisdom of the wise shall become as nought, and the understanding of the prudent shall be hid, and because the power of God shall be displayed, those who profess to know the truth but walk in deceit shall tremble with anger; but with signs and with wonders, with gifts and with healings, with the manifestations of the power of God, and with the Holy Ghost shall the hearts of the faithful be comforted. You have now beheld the power of God manifested and the power of Satan: you see that there is nothing that is desirable in the works of darkness; that they cannot bring happiness; that those who are overcome therewith are miserable, while on the other hand the righteous are blessed with a place in the kingdom of God where joy unspeakable surrounds them. There they rest beyond the power of the enemy of truth, where no evil can disturb them. The glory of God crowns them, and they continually feast upon his goodness and enjoy his smiles.

"Behold, notwithstanding you have seen this great display of power, by which you may ever be able to detect the evil one, yet I give unto you another sign, and when it comes to pass then know that the Lord is God and that he will fulfill his purposes, and that the knowledge which this record contains will go to every nation, and kindred, and tongue, and people under the whole heaven. This is the sign: when these things begin to be known, that is, when it is known that the Lord has shown you these things, the workers of iniquity will seek your overthrow: they will circulate falsehoods to destroy your reputation, and also will seek to take your life; but remember this, if you are faithful, and shall hereafter continue to keep the commandments of the Lord, you shall be preserved to bring these things forth; for in due time he will again give you a commandment to come and take them. When they are interpreted the Lord will give the holy priesthood to some, and they shall begin to proclaim this gospel and baptize by water, and after that they shall have power to give the Holy Ghost by the laying on of their hands.

"Then will persecution rage more and more; for the iniquities of men shall be revealed, and those who are not built upon the Rock will seek to overthrow this church; but it will increase the more opposed, and spread farther and farther, increasing in knowledge till they shall be sanctified and receive an inheritance where the glory of God will rest upon them; and when this takes place, and all things are prepared, the ten tribes of Israel will be revealed in the north country, whither they have been for a long season; and when this is fulfilled will be brought to pass that saying of the prophet—'And the Redeemer shall come to Zion, and unto them that turn from transgression in Jacob, saith the Lord.' But, notwithstanding the workers of iniquity shall seek your destruction the arm of the Lord will be extended, and you will be borne off conqueror, if you keep all his commandments. Your name shall be known among the nations, for the work which the Lord will perform by your hands shall cause the righteous to rejoice and the wicked to rage: with the one it shall be had in honor, and with the other in reproach; yet, with these it shall be a terror because of the great and marvelous work which shall follow the coming forth of this fullness of the gospel.

"Now, go thy way, remembering what the Lord has done for thee, and be diligent in keeping his commandments, and he will deliver thee from temptations and all the arts and devices of the wicked one. Forget not to pray, that thy mind may become strong, that when he shall manifest unto thee, thou mayest have power to escape the evil, and obtain these precious things."

Though I am unable to paint before the mind a perfect description of the scenery which passed before our brother, I think I have said enough to give you a field for reflection which may not be unprofitable. You see the great wisdom in God in leading him thus far, that his mind might begin to be more matured, and thereby be able to judge correctly the spirits. I do not say that he would not have obtained the record had he went according to the direction of the angel—I say that he would; but God, knowing all things from the beginning, began thus to instruct his servant. And in this it is plainly to be seen that the adversary of truth is not sufficient to overthrow the work of God. You will remember that I said two invisible powers were operating upon the mind of our brother while going to Cumorah. In this, then, I discover wisdom in the dealings of the Lord: it was impossible for any man to translate the Book of Mormon by the gift of God, and endure the afflictions, and temptations, and devices of Satan, without being overthrown, unless he had been previously benefited with a certain round of experience: and had our brother obtained the record the first time, not knowing how to detect the works of darkness, he might have been deprived of the blessing of sending forth the word of truth to this generation. Therefore, God knowing that Satan would thus lead his mind astray, began at that early hour, that when the full time should arrive, he might have a servant prepared to fulfill his purpose. So, however afflicting to his feelings this repulse might have been, he had reason to rejoice before the Lord and be thankful for the favors and mercies shown; that whatever other instruction was necessary to the accomplishing this great work, he had learned, by experience, how to discern between the spirit of Christ and the spirit of the devil.

From this time to September, 1827, few occurrences worthy of note transpired. As a fact to be expected, nothing of importance could be recorded concerning a generation in darkness. In the meantime, our brother of whom I have been speaking passed the time as others, in laboring for his support. But in consequence of certain false and slanderous reports which have been circulated, justice would require me to say something upon the private life of one whose character has been so shamefully traduced. By some he is said to have been a lazy, idle, vicious, profligate fellow. These I am prepared to contradict, and that too by the testimony of many persons with whom I have been intimately acquainted, and know to be individuals of the strictest veracity and unquestionable integrity. All these strictly and virtually agree in saying that he was an honest, upright, virtuous, and faithfully industrious young man. And those who say to the contrary can be influenced by no other motive than to destroy the reputation of one who never injured any man in either property or person.

While young, I have been informed he was afflicted with sickness; but I have been told by those for whom he has labored that he was a young man of truth and industrious habits. And I will add further that it is my conviction, if he never had been called to the exalted station in which he now occupies, he might have passed down the stream of time with ease and in respectability, without the foul and hellish tongue of slander ever being employed against him. It is no more than to be expected, I admit, that men of corrupt hearts will try to traduce his character and put a spot upon his name: indeed, this is according to the word of the angel; but this does not prohibit one from speaking freely of his merits, and contradicting those falsehoods—I feel myself bound so to do, and I know that my testimony, on this matter, will be received and believed while those who testify to the contrary are crumbled to dust, and their words swept away in the general mass of lies when God shall purify the earth!

Connected with this is the character of the family: and on this I say as I said concerning the character of our brother—I feel myself bound to defend the innocent always when opportunity offers. Had not those who are notorious for lies and dishonesty also assailed the character of the family, I should pass over them here in silence; but now I shall not forbear. It has been industriously circulated that they were dishonest, deceitful, and vile. On this I have the testimony of responsible persons, who have said and will say, that this is basely false; and besides, a personal acquaintance for seven years has demonstrated that all the difficulty is, they were once poor (yet industrious) and have now, by the help of God, arisen to note, and their names are like to (indeed they will) be handed down to posterity, and had among the righteous. They are industrious, honest, virtuous, and liberal to all. This is their character; and though many take advantage of their liberality, God will reward them; but this is the fact, and this testimony shall shine upon the records of the Saints, and be recorded on the archives of heaven to be read in the day of eternity, when the wicked and perverse, who have vilely slandered them without cause or provocation, reap their reward with the unjust, where there is weeping, wailing, and gnashing of teeth!—if they do not repent.

Soon after this visit to Cumorah, a gentleman from the south part of the State (Chenango County) employed our brother as a common laborer, and accordingly he visited that section of the country; and had he not been accused of digging down all, or nearly so, the mountains of Susquehannah, or causing others to do it by some art of necromancy, I should leave this, for the present, unnoticed.

You will remember, in the meantime, that those who seek to vilify his character say that he has always been notorious for his idleness. This gentleman, whose name is [Josiah] Stowel, resided in the town of Bainbridge, on or near the headwaters of the Susquehannah river.

Some forty miles south, or down the river, in the town of Harmony, Susquehannah County, Pa., is said to be a cave or subterraneous recess, whether entirely formed by art or not I am uninformed, neither does this matter; but such is said to be the case, when a company of Spaniards, a long time since, when the country was uninhabited by white settlers, excavated from the bowels of the earth ore, and coined a large quantity of money; after which they secured the cavity and evacuated, leaving a part still in the cave, purposing to return at some distant period. A long time elapsed and this account came from one of the individuals who was first engaged in this mining business, the country was pointed out and the spot minutely described. This, I believe, is the substance, so far as my memory serves, though I shall not pledge my veracity for the correctness of the account as I have given. Enough, however, was credited of the Spaniard's story to excite the belief of many that there was a fine sum of the precious metal being coined in this subterraneous vault, among whom was our employer; and accordingly our brother was required to spend a few months with some others in excavating the earth, in pursuit of this treasure.

While employed here he became acquainted with the family of Isaac Hale, of whom you read in several of the productions of those who have sought to destroy the validity of the Book of Mormon. It may be necessary hereafter to refer you more particularly to the conduct of this family, as their influence has been considerably exerted to destroy the reputation of our brother, probably because he married a daughter of the same contrary to some of their wishes, and in connection with this to certain statements of some others of the inhabitants of that section of country. But in saying this I do not wish to be understood as uttering aught against Mrs. Smith (formerly Emma Hale). She has most certainly evinced a decidedly correct mind and uncommon ability of talent and judgement, in a manifest willingness to fulfill, on her part, that passage in sacred writ—"and they twain shall be one flesh"—by accompanying her husband, against the wishes and advice of her relatives, to a land of strangers: and however I may deprecate their actions, can say in justice, her character stands as fair for morality, piety, and virtue as any in the world.

Though you may say this is a digression from the subject proposed, I trust I shall be indulged, for the purpose of satisfying many who have heard so many slanderous reports that they are led to believe them true because they are not contradicted; and besides, this generation are determined to oppose every item in the form or under the pretense of revelation, unless it comes through a man who has always been more pure than Michael the great prince; and as this is the fact, and my opposers have put me to the necessity, I shall be more prolix, and have no doubt, before I give up the point, shall prove to your satisfaction, and to that of every man, that the translator of the Book of Mormon is worthy the appellation of a seer and a prophet of the Lord. In this I do not pretend that he is not a man subject to passion like other men, beset with infirmities and encompassed with weaknesses; but if he is, all men were so before him, and a pretense to the contrary would argue a more than mortal, which would at once destroy the whole system of the religion of the Lord Jesus; for he anciently chose the weak to overcome the strong, the foolish to confound the wise (I mean considered so by this world), and by the foolishness of preaching to save those who believe.

On the private character of our brother I need add nothing further, at present, previous to his obtaining the records of the Nephites, only that while in that country, some very officious person complained of him as a disorderly person, and brought him before the authorities of the country; but there being no cause of action he was honorably acquitted. From this time forward he continued to receive instructions concerning the coming forth of the fullness of the gospel, from the mouth of the heavenly messenger, until he was directed to visit again the place where the records were deposited.

For the present I close, with a thankful heart that I am permitted to see thousands rejoicing in the assurance of the promises of the Lord, confirmed unto them through the obedience of the everlasting covenant.

As ever, your brother in the Lord Jesus.

OLIVER COWDERY.

www.ingramcontent.com/pod-product-compliance
Lightning Source LLC
Chambersburg PA
CBHW031604040426
42452CB00006B/405